Essence of Egypt,

Discover the best of the Land of the Pharaohs with travel tips and advice from top travelers.

By Thomas Langstaff

Table of Contents

Table of Contents

Introduction

This guide is for the tourist who is interested in the history of Egypt but only has a limited time to visit and explore the country. Many people have seen the pyramids and want to know more about the ancient Egyptians who built them. The pyramids at Giza were built around 2500BC and are rightly one of the seven wonders of the world. Much has happened of historical interest during the following 4500 years up until today! The pyramids are not the only sites of interest in Egypt. There are many other sites visited on this tour all of which pre-date the collapse of the Roman empire in about 500AD. As this covers a range of 3000 years we are talking about a lot of history. You should understand that the ancient Egyptians were also ancient to the Romans.

Chapter 1: - Experience Egypt

Why Egypt?

When I think back to my favorite childhood movies, Disney's Aladdin was always a real stand out. After I visited Egypt for the first time, my brother and I decided to watch Aladdin together on the plane trip home. (We had been to some other middle eastern countries too)

Till this day, I still remember how special watching that movie was to me after having the shared experience of visiting Egypt with my family.

What to Eat and Drink in Egypt

Egyptian Beverages

One of the most important parts of any Egyptian meal is the beverage. Fresh fruit juice and milk-based beverages are the most popular and common types. You'll also find that many people enjoy imported alcoholic beverages or freshly squeezed juices, though they are relatively uncommon in Egypt. You can't go wrong with a glass of freshly squeezed lemon juice either! The water used to make these drinks is traditionally from the Nile River, so it will taste different from bottled water. Before drinking any water, make sure you know where it came from and if it's safe.

Egyptian Drinks

1. Coffee: the most widely consumed beverage in Egypt! The country is known for its Arabica beans, and old-fashioned drip-style coffee pots are a common sight in cafes. Coffee must be served with sugar, with one cube being typical. Coffee shops are a social hub and a great place to meet people.
2. Karkade: delicious, sweet, black tea made from hibiscus flowers. You'll find it in most restaurants, but it's also quite sweet so if you're not a fan of sugar it may not be for you.

Milk-based Beverages

1. Tahina: a spicy sesame-based drink made from fresh-ground sesame seeds. It has a much stronger taste than the more common ma'a tahina, which is made from dried sesame seeds and contains less sugar. The sweet variety is like hummus and often served with pita.
2. Lebanese Milk Tea: a favorite for tourists, this tea is light, sweet and refreshing. It's served as it sounds, with small amounts of milk added to black tea leaves. You'll find it all over Egypt in tourist areas like Luxor and Aswan.

Beer and Wine: the country has three alcoholic beverages that are quite popular: beer, wine and spirits. Beer is brewed by most people in Egypt, though the brewing process is not that common due to the high cost of equipment. Bottled beer is a better alternative to drinking from a keg. Wines made from grapes are also common and can be found in most restaurants as well as supermarkets, and include such varieties as rose, table wine and dessert wines. Spirits are made from corn or fruit but vary strongly in flavor.

1. Rice with Meat and Beans: an Egyptian meal staple, this dish is typically served at lunchtime. The rice is cooked with chunks of beef or chicken in a tomato sauce. It's normally served with bread to mop up the sauce and is a very filling dish for travelers in Egypt.
2. Turkish Coffee: dark, thick coffee usually served after dinner, Turkish coffee is a mild-flavored brew that's easy to like. It's served hot with either sugar or a cinnamon-honey syrup and may sometimes be mixed with milk.

Egyptian Food

Eggs are very popular in Egypt, especially in the north of the country. The eggs of Egyptian fowl can be found at most markets and are often fried or poached. Other dishes are made with these same birds, such as stuffed vegetables and whole chickens. Cod is also known to be a commonly eaten fish in Egypt, though it is sometimes cooked like chicken.

Egypt Best Historical Sights

Egypt is a country that has contributed much to human culture and civilization. One of the most fascinating aspects of Egypt's legacy is the vast number of ancient sites, from pyramids to tombs, scattered across its desert terrain. These archaeological sites are filled with secrets and hidden treasures.

The best archaeological sites in Egypt are relatively easy to reach. Whether by plane, train, or car, it is easiest to reach these sites from Cairo. Air travel is available from Cairo International Airport (CAI), which is located just outside the city. The airport has connections to major cities across Canada and the United States with direct service offered by KLM, Delta, and Air Transat.

The best time to visit Egypt is during the winter months of October through May when flight prices are more reasonable. The airport has two terminals and a total of four runways, with a parking lot that can accommodate up to 12 planes.

Once you arrive in Egypt, one of the first things to see is the Pyramids of Giza. These man-made pyramids were constructed roughly 4,500 years ago by Pharaohs Khufu, Khafre and Menkaure and have been one of the most famous Ancient Egyptian archeological sites since they were first built.

Egypt's Top Outdoor Adventures

1) The Great Pyramids of Giza.

2) The Mosque of Muhammad Ali.

3) Heading up the Nile on a felucca boat to explore villages and temples.

4) Swimming in one of the Red Sea's numerous excellent beaches like Brothers, Dahab, or Marsa Alam.

5) Climbing Mount Sinai for some spectacular views and climbing experience for beginners too advanced climbers.

6) Climbing Mount Sinai from the St. Catherine's Monastery side.

7) Snorkeling on one of the Red Sea's many excellent reefs and seeing the abundant marine life.

8) Golfing at one of Egypt's numerous golf courses like The City of Dreams, Marsa Matrouh, El Quseir or in Luxor at Karnak.

9) Sailing down the Nile on the traditional and highly comfortable felucca boat.

10) Visiting one of Egypt's many museums like the Egyptian Museum in Cairo, Khan el Khalili Bazaar or one of the many entertaining Souks (markets).

11) Visit an active archaeological site and see an excavating team at work like Aswan , Kom Ombo, Saqqara or ancient Alexandria.

What To Read And Watch

Egypt's cinema scene has experienced a revival since the 2011 Egyptian revolution. The film Elham Ahmed was made by an Egyptian woman and is about a woman's tribulations with her mother-in-law. Some of the most recent films created in Egypt are Fahd, The Scar, Banat Asha'ar, and Zamalek 1914. Egypt has also won awards in international film festivals.

- Middle East
- Culture and society
- Sports and leisure
- Retail and services
- Business and economy

- Inventors and scientists
- Works and literature

The publishing industry in Egypt has traditionally been very large, due largely to the ready availability of editors and print facilities during the 19th century. Currently, although the book market is still quite active, its condition is far from healthy. Bookstores are scarce outside of Cairo, and the greater availability of books on paper has not been accompanied by a comparable rise in demand for books.

Egypt's official languages are Arabic and English. It is compulsory for pupils to study four different languages: Arabic, English, French, and German. Only a handful of Egyptian children learn as many as four languages in school (the number of who actually do are not known).

The Egyptian dialect of Arabic is a MSA (Modern Standard Arabic) variety, which is different in form from the colloquial dialect(s). Colloquial Egyptian Arabic includes numerous loanwords from Turkish and French, as well as words that are unique to Egypt.

Chapter 2: - Travel Smart

Contact with Home

Going abroad means finding the best way to stay in touch with your family and friends at home.

Mobile Phones

- The cheapest way to stay in contact with home is to buy an Egyptian SIM card.
- Calls are significantly cheaper than if you used your own mobile provider from home on roaming rates.
- Make sure your mobile phone is unlocked so SIM cards from any network can be used.
- You can test this before you leave for Egypt by replacing your SIM card with a friend's SIM card as long as it is from a different network provider.

If you're able to make calls with your friend's SIM card then your phone is unlocked and it will be fine to use in Egypt.

If your phone is locked, you can call your mobile provider and pay a fee to have it unlocked which is usually cheaper than buying a new phone to use in Egypt.

If you have an Apple iPhone, be sure to get it unlocked at an Apple shop. Also, make sure that after you unlock it you don't make the mistake of syncing it to your computer otherwise it will become locked again.

Wi-Fi Hotspots

For a comprehensive list of Wi-Fi Hotspots in Egypt, visit the following URL:

http://www.wi-fihotspotsdirectory.com/Wi-Fi-Hotspots-In-Egypt-67.html

Helpful phrases

English Arabic translation (written in English)

One Wahed

Two Etneyn

Three T alaata

Four Arbaa'a

Five Khamsa

Six Sita

Seven Sabaa'a

Eight T amanya

Nine Tes'aa

Ten Ashara

Eleven Hedaa'shar

Twelve Etnaa'shar

Thirteen Talataa'shar

Fourteen Arbaa'taa'shar

Fifteen Khamestaa'shar

Sixteen Sitaa'shar

Seventeen Sabaa'taa'shar

Eighteen Tamentaa'shar

Nineteen Tese'taa'shar

Twenty Eshreen

Twenty one Wahed we eshreen

Twenty two Etneyn we eshreen

Thirty T alateen

Forty Arbaa'een

Fifty Khamseen

Sixty Siteen

Seventy Sab'een

Eighty T amaneen

Ninety T es'een

One hundred Meya

Two hundred Meyteen

Three hundred Tolta meya

Four hundred Arbaa' meya

Egyptian Pound Gneyh (masri)

No La'

Yes Aywa

Thank you Shokran.

Please Law samaht (m)

 Law samahte (f)

Hello Marhabaa

Welcome Ahlan wa sahlan

Good morning Sabaah el kheir

Good afternoon / good evening Masaa el kheir

How are you? Izayak? (m)

 Izayik (f)

Fine, thank you Tamam, shokran.

Excuse me Law samaht (or) Baa'd iznak (m)

 Law samahte (or) Baa'd iznik (f)

This one Dah (m)

 Di (f)

How much is this? Bkaam dah? (m)

 Bkaam di? (f)

No, that's too expensive. La', dah keteer.

Ill buy it for... Hakhdo be...

OK Mashi

What time is it please? Alsaa'aa kaam, law samaht? (m)

Alsaa'aa kaam, law samahte? (f)

Where are the bathrooms please? Alhamaam feyn, law samaht? (m)

Alhamaam feyn, law samahte? (f)

Things to Do/Get Before You Leave for Egypt

As exciting as traveling to a new country can be, it's can also be equally stressful.

Especially those last couple of days before your trip when you're worried whether you have everything ready or if you've forgotten to pack something.

The following checklist will hopefully make those last few days before your trip less stressful and more organized.

Item	Details	✓
Visa	•Visas cost $15 US / person •Payable when you arrive in Egypt •See the section 'Arriving at the Airport in Egypt'	
Travel Documents	For a comprehensive list check out : http://www.traveldocs.com/eg/	
Copies of Documents	•Passport •Credit cards •Other important documents	

	Use Evernote* to save documents online. Accessible wherever you have an internet connection. *Evernote website http://www.evernote.com/	
Travel Insurance	Don't leave home or book a flight without it. Many credit cards include travel insurance. Contact your bank for the details.	
Transport Bookings	Book transfers from the airport to your hotel so you don't get lost on arrival.	
Embassy	Know where your embassy is - just in case. Here are a few: British: http://ukinegypt.fco.gov.uk/en/ U.S: http://cairo.usembassy.gov/ Australian: http://www.egypt.embassy.gov.au/caro/home.html	

Student / Youth Card	Anyone under 26 can get one (whether a student or not) This will get you great discounts.	
Earplugs	Handy wherever you travel in the world, but especially in busy Cairo.	
Sunscreen	While it's sold in Egypt, its expensive. So, pack a bottle unless you don't mind paying the higher price.	
Clothes	Have appropriate clothing ready to wear when you get there. See chapter 'Clothing: What to Wear and What Not To Wear' for more details.	
Camera	Essential for any trip!	
Sunglasses & Hat	The sun is blinding, and not only do you risk getting a sun stroke, but it can leave your eyes feeling very dry and sore.	
Eye Drops	A lot of tourists complain about their eyes feeling too dry/sore/red. Bring moisturizing eye drops just	

	in case.	
Power Adapter	Egypt uses 220 volt and plugs are two prongs rounded.	

Getting Here And Around

Below is a simplified guide that takes you through the process of arriving at Cairo Airport for the first time, or any other airport in Egypt. It explains everything you need to do from the moment you arrive at the airport.

Immigration formalities

The first thing you're going to have to deal with at the airport, and like most airports around the world, is passport control; so get your visa fees ready ($15 for most foreigners) and your passport out, ready to be stamped for entry.

- You'll be asked to fill in a landing card (usually orange in color) with the following details:
- Flight number: The number of the flight you came on (find this on your boarding pass).
- Coming from: Write the name of the city (and country) you travelled from.
- Name: Write your full name (as shown in your passport).
- Date of birth: dd/mm/yyyy
- Passport number and type: Write your passport number and type of passport (usually your passport type is "normal" unless otherwise specified).

- Address in Egypt: If you've already found an apartment you're renting out, write the address. If you're staying at a hotel, just write the hotel name and include the city, for example, Sheraton-Heliopolis or Sheraton - Giza. If you don't know where you're staying yet, just give them the name of any hotel (it doesn't really matter).
- You'll then be asked to tick the purpose of your stay, tick travel or other as applicable.
- If your child is on your passport, then you will be asked to write his or her name and date of birth with you on the same landing card. However, if your child has his or her own passport, you will need to fill a separate landing card for him / her.

Getting Your Luggage

One of the best things about Egyptian airports is that their trolleys are completely free!

- You don't need to worry about having change to unlock the trolleys.
- Each trolley fits up to 4 bags, depending on the size of your bags of course.
- There are larger trolleys that fit up to 20 bags.
- › These can be rented for about 30 EGP (Egyptian Pounds) or $5.
- You'll also have to tip the worker who pushes the trolley (around 5 to 10 EGP). Customs

After you get your luggage gathered, you still must go through customs before you get to walk out into the streets of Egypt.

- The officer at customs will ask to see your passport, and s/he may even ask you to open your bags.
- Don't hesitate and follow his or her instructions right away to avoid further delay.
- The maximum local currency you're allowed to take out of Egypt is 5,000 EGP.
- There is no limit on the amount of hard currency you bring with you but amounts over $10,000 should usually be announced upon arrival.

No Visa Requirement?

Nationals of some countries (British, American, etc.) don't require a visa when traveling to some locations in Egypt, namely Sharm El Sheikh, Dahab, Nuweiba and Taba resorts, as long as they only intend to stay there for up to 14 days. If this is the case you will receive free entry permission stamp upon arrival.

Should you wish to extend your stay or travel outside the above-mentioned areas even within your 14 day permitted stay, a visa will need to be obtained allowing you to stay for up to 1 month.

A lot of tourists who travel to Sinai without a visa obtain a visa from Sharm El Sheikh airport so they can travel around freely.

Note: If you want to extend your visa within Egypt, you will can visit the Egyptian Passport and Immigration Offices

Don't Forget

- Change currency into Egyptian pounds before leaving the airport

 ‣ There are plenty of banks inside the airport.

- Be sure to check out the duty-free shop in the airport

Great Itinerary

Day 1

Fly to Luxor.

Day 2

Visit the temple at Karnak.

Visit the temple at Luxor.

Visit the Winter Palace hotel for a drink.

If you have not pre-booked your Nile cruise, visit the travel agents outside the Winter Palace.

Day 3

Hire a Taxi for the day but negotiate a price before you set off.

Go to the ticket office and buy tickets for Carter's house and the Worker's Village.

Visit The Valley of the Kings.

Visit Howard Carter's house.

Visit Hatshepsut's temple - Deir el-Bari.

Visit The Workers Village - Deir el-Medina.

If you want to climb El-Qorn on day 6 ask your hotel to find you an experienced guide.

Day 4

Catch a service bus to the Colossi of Memnon. This will be very cheap if you pay the same fare as the locals.

After viewing the Colossi take the opportunity to see the archeological work underway on the site of the temple of Amenhotep III.

Walk to the ticket office and buy tickets for the following tombs of the nobles: TT96 Senheffer, TT52 Nakht and TT69 Menna.

At the Tombs of the Nobles ask a guide on the site to take you to the tombs.

Day 5

Use the service bus to the ticket office.

Visit The Ramesseum.

Visit Medinet Habu.

These sites are an easy walk from the ticket office.

Day 6

Catch the service bus to the ticket office and cross the road to the Marsam hotel.

Walk on to climb to the top of El-Qorn (Optional) - This is only for experienced walkers with a head for heights and will take the whole day. Do not attempt this walk on your own. Take a guide familiar with the path and use the route passing the Monastery.

Alternatively take the opportunity to rest and have lunch at the Marsam hotel. This will give you the chance to sit on the terrace and enjoy the view of the fertile farmland in the Nile valley.

Day 7

Call your hotel in Aswan to book a place on a guided tour to Abu Simbel on day 11. An alternative is to use a taxi.

Visit Dendera.

Join the cruise ship in the evening.

Day 8

Visit the Temple of Khum at Esna.

Visit the Temple of Horus at Edfu.

Spend the night on the ship.

Day 9

Visit the Temple of Sobek and Horus at Kom Ombo.

Spend the night on the ship.

Day 10

Disembark at Aswan early in the morning.

Visit the Temple of Isis at Philae.

Visit the Unfinished Obelisk.

Take lunch at the Old Cataract Hotel and enjoy the view over the first cataract, a shallow section of the river with many rocks.

Visit the Nubian Museum.

Day 11

Make a very early start and visit Abu Simbel. Organised tours depart at around 3am.

Day 12

Fly to Cairo.

Visit the Souk for shopping. (optional)

Day 13

Visit the Pyramids at Giza.

Day 14

Visit the Egyptian Museum.

Depart for Home.

Essentials for Visiting Egypt

Dress

Essentially a conventional society with overwhelming strict traditions, any dress uncovering portions of the body may be disapproved of, similar to shorts or sleeveless tops. This applies both to people. Ladies need to observe the need to cover cleavage and shouldn't favor tight-fitting clothing. Long streaming skirts or maxi dresses would be great. Moreover, a headscarf/wrap or light sweatshirt to cover shoulders would be helpful. The head ought to be covered while entering a mosque.

As for strolling, however shoes are worn by local ladies, for visiting travelers, agreeable shoes would be more useful taking into account the road conditions, as lopsided pathways and nonattendance of tidiness. Shoes are likewise satisfactory. One will be expected to take off shoes while entering a position of Islamic love.

Money

Initially, cash bills are for the most part oily and malodorous because of regular use; hand sanitizer will, in this way, be valuable. Furthermore, consistently convey little category notes and coins while branching out. The act of tips, called 'baksheesh' is generally predominant. For any assistance, whether cab drivers, watchmen, servers, or those giving bathroom tissue in open bathrooms, or anybody assisting you with stacking or dump stuff, will expect it.

Tourists are helped to remember the presence of tricksters. One could experience them just subsequent to getting off the plane.

As in other vacationer places in the Middle East, one would go over numerous who might offer spontaneous help or tips for transport or shopping.

 Usually, they'd profess to accompany you to a known shop of their cousin or deal their administrations as the best aide in light of sensible tip, or 'baksheesh.' It would be more secure just to overlook them with much obliged. Many visits recommended by them are overrated. The more secure way is to venture out in a gathering to kill such traps.

Trains

The train station for going to Luxor is Giza. Many trains leave from Ramses station too. There are 3 classes: Express, Ordinary, and Local. Express trains are agreeable and less swarmed. Delays are normal. The principle courses which have more recurrence of trains are Cairo Alexandria, Cairo-Luxor, and Luxor-Aswan. The Cairo-Luxor-Aswan trains are controlled by Watania. Train appointments can be made on the web. Other mainline trains are controlled by the Egyptian rail routes. Direct trains are airconditioned and have five star mentors, mostly utilized by vacationers and princely Egyptians. Cairo-Luxor (313 miles) airconditioned compartment for two expenses $110, single $80, and takes almost 12 hrs.

Roads

There is a decent organization of streets that interfaces the significant urban areas. The street conditions in non-metropolitan regions may not be in great circumstances, rutted, or with broke down patches. The optional streets are not terrible, however one would track down them with free sand, mud, or rock. Because of the level landscape, the long street travel is in straight stretches.

Driving through the rustic regions, one ought to be on the consistent post for hindrances wrongfully laid across the street by local people. These can harm the suspension of the vehicle. Driving external Cairo, one will observe police check-posts requesting reports like visa and license.

Buses

For public vehicle in Cairo, individuals use cable cars and transports worked by government transport organizations. The administrations are successive between 05.30 a.m. until 01.00 around evening time. Notwithstanding, packing is an aggravation, particularly during the busy times when even it is challenging to stand space. The course and the name of the objective are shown in Arabic on the front. The guide (kumsari) gathers the toll inside the transport. Smoking isn't permitted.

There are between city administrations, however no immediate transport administration among Cairo and Luxor; it's through Hurghada, tedious, and isn't fitting for the travelers. The significant distance administrations are given by five organizations serving their separate areas. Eastern Delta serves the Canal region, Mansurah, and Damietta; Middle Delta to Kafr al-Shaykh and Manufiyyah, Tanta; Western Delta to Damanhur, Alexandria; and Sinai Bus Company serves Sinai regions. These organizations have their workplaces in Cairo.

The transport administrations are of three kinds. In the first place, those calling at each station in the between city with less stops. Or on the other hand the express class, offering better solace, similar to a saved seat, cleaner latrine, and tidbits. The exclusive class has cooling, yet others play with open windows that can allow in a ton of dust.

Taxis

Hailed by calling 'taksi' with a lifted hand, these are in the principle cities.

The charge meter is at the front of the dashboard and runs according to the rate supported by the public authority. The endorsed passage is additionally appropriate to go external Cairo city. In the city, a limousine 'Misr' administration is likewise worked by the public authority organization nonstop. Somewhat more costly however more solid, it very well may be reached by phone on Cairo number 2599813. It will likewise offer an assistance to take the guest outside Cairo.

Car Rentals

These can be recruited through the lodging or the traveler organizations; the tax relies upon the kind of vehicle. An International Driving License is legitimate for six months.

Carriages

Carriages are a magnificent approach to seeing the common urban communities and visiting distant regions. Their positions are typically tracked down near the station, and the drivers frequently understand the region better than the cabbies; that's what another benefit is albeit more slow, they can frequently travel where the taxi cannot.

Airport to City

The overall white and yellow taxicabs have toll meters while numerous others run on fixed courses and admissions. It is generally fitting to check from the inn the considerable lot you ought to pay for a taxi ride and set the passage prior to getting into it. As an aide, a 3-km taxi ride in Cairo could be between EP 2.50 - 3.00. There are transport administrations between the air terminal and the city with admissions running between EP 25 and 100; somewhere in the range of 65 and 470 for the "limousine administrations," which are like taxicabs however with fixed costs relying upon your objective and the degree of solace you want. The public transport administration from the air terminal to the downtown area has a proper passage of Piaster 70. The metro ride inside the city is generally sensible at Piasters 20-50.

Uber administrations began in Cairo and Alexandria a couple of years back. These have become well known and are probably going to grow to different urban communities. Cairo alone brags of in excess of 90,000 Uber drivers.

Security and Law and Order

Despite reports of illegal intimidation in the adjoining nations, Egypt has delighted in relative harmony and soundness for a really long time. Before, there have been psychological militant assaults against the travelers; the fundamental ones are the 1993 blast on a vacationer transport at Giza Pyramids, the 1993 killing of American and French sightseers in Cairo, the 1997 Luxor slaughter killing 62 travelers, the 2004 besieging of French flight that carried French vacationers from Sharm El-Sheik and the 2004 bombings at traveler lodgings in Sinai. However the public authority has presented safety efforts, the vacationers need to avoid potential risk like not branching out around evening time in far-away places, particularly in the desert. The

American and British tourism warnings deny travel to North Sinai and just fundamental travel to South Sinai. Vacationer places like Sharm El Sheik are safer. Apart from psychological oppressor viciousness, Egypt experienced critical political unrest beginning around 2011, influencing the homegrown climate. This has here and there elaborate savage fights and aggravations, which have brought about various deaths.

Protests, walks, and exhibitions have happened across Egypt in the new past. Assuming that you become mindful of any close by fights, walks, or shows, you ought to create some distance from the prompt region as the air could change rapidly and all of a sudden. Police have recently utilized water cannons, poisonous gas, birdshot, and live ammo for swarm control.

Foreigners participating in any type of political action or exercises incredulous of the public authority might be in danger of detention.

Road mishaps are normal due to the unfortunate street conditions and traffic rule infringement, and, obviously, perilous driving. It would be more secure to keep away from street travel around evening time, particularly outside the primary urban areas and resorts. Ensure you have satisfactory insurance.

If you are going rough terrain, utilize a certified aide and get suitable licenses from the Ministry of Interior. A vacationer police grant is expected for outsiders traveling south from Nuweiba towards Abu Ghaloum and furthermore east to the Colored Canyon, and clearly for other explicit areas of Egypt.

The crime percentage in Egypt is for the most part low, yet throughout the long term, guests have occasionally experienced outfitted thefts, muggings (remembering for taxis), rapes, and break-ins to convenience and vehicles. Be careful with pickpockets and sack snatchers too.

Chapter 3: - Cairo

It is necessary to fly to Cairo for the last stage of this trip. It is a good way to end the journey as you can visit two wonderful sights. Cairo is not the most pleasant of cities. The traffic in particular poses a significant danger. Only those with strong nerves can cross the road! However, it is worth braving the city to see the Pyramids at Giza and to visit the Egyptian museum and in particular the treasures of Tutankhamen.

I recommend using a good hotel which may cost a little more, but the staff will be able to ensure that your visit is enjoyable and safe. Always take advice from the staff particularly on whether it is advisable to visit the Egyptian museum. The end of January is not a good time to visit given the increased tension on the anniversary of the revolution. It is also important to only use taxis recommended by the hotel, otherwise you might suffer a long detour visiting bazaars and shops you have no interest in.

The Pyramids of Giza

Everyone who visits Egypt will want to visit the pyramids and marvel at the size of the construction. It is not known exactly how these enormous structures were constructed. Although they appear to be rough stone the facing stones on the top section of the Pyramid of Khafre, shows that they were actually clad with limestone and smooth. It comes as a surprise to many people just how close the city is to the site. You come to understand that all the photos you see of the pyramids are cleverly taken to avoid the view of the city! The Sphinx can also be seen on the same site although it does show the ravages of time. It is not entirely complete, and the missing beard can be seen in the British Museum in London.

Old Cairo (Coptic Cairo)

The Coptic Museum in this city houses one of Egypt's best collections of Coptic art and is a source of knowledge on early Christian Egypt. Beautiful examples of Coptic architecture can be found next door at the Hanging Church from the ninth century. The church was initially constructed over the Roman gate towers, hence its name, and underwent a significant rebuilding project in the ninth century.

The Church of St. Sergius and Bacchus, where local legend has it that the Virgin Mary, Baby Jesus, and family sought refuge during King Herod's killing of male infants, is the main highlight of a trip to this neighborhood for many Christian visitors. The Ben Ezra Synagogue, located further into the neighborhood, is claimed to have been constructed close to the location where the newborn Moses was discovered among the reeds. The Amr Ibn al-As Mosque, which was the first mosque constructed in Egypt, is located nearby.

The quickest way to get to Coptic Cairo is by riding the Cairo Metro to the Mar Girgis stop.

Sharia Mar Girgis is situated south of Downtown.

Budget Hotels

Most hotels have shown the price for a double room, which might change according to the seasons.

One can visit Hostelworld to look for the largest inventory of hostel accommodation. Budget travelers also use Booking.com to find the cheapest rates for guesthouses and hotels.

Finding a hotel without a reservation may not be a problem, but reserving one for the first night will be convenient.

Many hotels provide airport pick up, free, or if the stay is more than 2 nights.

Rooms may not be spacious enough to fit an extra crib for babies.

The budget hostels offer bare facilities, some on a sharing basis, all under $20 per night. In Cairo, some of these are Wake Up Cairo, Freedom Hostel, Dahab Hostel, Cecilia Hostel, One Season, King Tut Hostel.

Cairo

The Best View Pyramids Hotel, Giza district, 1050 meters from Giza Pyramid,

13 Gamal Abd Nasser Street, Nazlet El Samman, Al Haram, Giza, E.g., Cairo, $50 with breakfast.

Pyramids Village Inn (Dr. Eglal Mohamed St, Cairo), 1.2 km from the Giza Pyramids and a 40-minute drive from the airport, $45 with breakfast.

Atlas International Hotel, located within 25 minutes walking distance from Al-Azhar Park, at 2 Mohamed Roushdi St, 25 minute-walk from Al-Azhar Park. $37

Pyramids Eyes Hotel, near Dokki metro station, $57 with breakfast.

Pearl Hotel, Maadi, located near The District Mall, 32 Rd,7 Intersection of Rd.82, offers 48 rooms with sea views, $69 with breakfast.

The Central Paris Hostel, 5 Talaat Harb St, offers a golf course, $62 with breakfast.

Maskadi Pyramids View, 28 Gamal Abd El Nasir Nazlet Alsman, Giza District, near Meidum Pyramid, $28.

The 3-star Great Pyramid Inn in Giza district, 14 Abou Al Hool Al Seiaji Pyramids Plateau, $68 with breakfast.

Milano Hotel, 2-star, in Dokki district, $ 43 with breakfast, a few minutes' walk from Nasser underground station.

Miami Cairo Hostel, 34 Talaat Harb St, near Egyptian Museum, $ 24.

Grand Palace Hotel, 14 Champollion Rd, 1.7 km from Islamic Art Museum, $ 37.

Sufi Pyramids Inn, 19 Abou Al Hool Al Seiahi St, Giza, $ 39Cairo,

Giza Pyramids Inn, 6 Sphinx St, Pyramids Giza, $ 61 with breakfast.

Nour Hostel, 34 Talaat Hzab St., Dokki district, 20-minute walking distance from Cairo Tower, $27 with breakfast.

New City Hotel, 5 Taalat Harb St, Tahrir Sq, Dokki district, close to Tahrir Square, $34.

Victoria Hotel, 66, El Gomhoria St, near Cairo Ramses Station, $36.

Tahrir Plaza, close to Liberation Square, Tahrir Square, 19 Meret Basha St. $57.

Sunshine Pyramids View Hotel, Nazlet El Semman, Gamal Abfd El Abd El Nasr St, $ 27.

Marvel Stone Hotel, 6 Gerier St, Nazlet El Semman, Giza, $ 61 with breakfast.

Abdeen Palace Hotel, 2 Sabry Abo Alam St, downtown Cairo, $ 35.

Cairo Paradise Hotel, 41 Sherif St, Al Fawalah, Abdeen (tel:20-2-23964220) $15-20.

Cairo Moon, 28 Adly Street، Bab Al Louq, Abdeen, (tel:20-2-23905119) $20.

23.Cairo Inn, 6 Talaat Harb Square, downtown Cairo, (tel:+20-100-077-3210) $30.

24.Cairo View, 44 A Talaat Harb St, Downtown Cairo, (tel: +20 100 801 64426), $20.

Chapter 4: - Alexandria

Alexandria is a city in Egypt, with the population of 4.7 million people, on the western bank of the Mediterranean Sea. It is also known as The City of a Thousand Trabels and Smiling Faces because it was founded by Alexander the Great in 331 BC. Within Alexandria are numerous important historical sites including royal palaces, monasteries and temples that today attract many visitors to their archaeological sites.

Alexandria was founded by Alexander the Great, who was Greek King of Macedonia. He built the city on the western bank of the Mediterranean Sea to be close to a major water supply. When Alexander died in 323 BC, his second wife and son took over Alexandria and made it their capital. It was at that time that Ptolemy I Soter began construction on a new palace. The palace became known as "The Lagoon". The palace of Alexandria is only one of several buildings in the city that are part of the UNESCO World Heritage List. It is also one of the most preserved buildings in the Ptolemaic dynasty.

When Cleopatra took control of Egypt, she moved her society to Alexandria, because it was a major port. She built large temples to honor herself as a goddess, including one that was a remodeled temple at Dendera. It took eighteen years to finish this temple.

After Cleopatra's death in 30 BC, Egypt was conquered by Romans. Alexandria became a major port for the Roman Empire and gained the status of a model city. It was given an exceptional number of architectural projects under Roman rule, including a lighthouse that was one of the tallest in the world at that time.

Downtown And Raml Station.

Downtown Raml station is an important place for the citizens in Egypt. It's one of the most crowded places at the time of rush hours. People use it to go everywhere and to travel in different directions, so it fully deserves this title. This is because people are looking for comfort, safety, and reliability from public transportation systems; however, there are some complaints about their service which causes some citizenries not to trust them anymore with traveling inside Egypt.

There are many ways to get to Downtown Raml station. For example, you can go by bus, metro or trolleybus in downtown Cairo. You can also use one of the numerous private taxi companies that offer service in downtown Cairo. This is because they do not have enough riders so they have to use private transport vehicles, which is sometimes a problem with safety concerns. The best and most comfortable way is the metro which serves you fast and safely and it goes everywhere else. The metro is the most popular public transportation system in Egypt because of the fact it's cheap and easy to use.

The Downtown Raml station has a lot of flaws especially when it comes to safety concerns. The most obvious and dangerous issue is the Metro's lack of security for passengers. This can be a big reason for rape, robbery, and molestation cases. Another problem is its old infrastructure which causes delays on their services. Metro Raml station is mostly crowded for the time of rush hours and people usually wait for hours to get a place in the train.

Temple and Statues of Luxor

Southern Egypt's Luxor is a city located on the east bank of the Nile River. It is located on the site of the ancient city of Thebes, which served as the capital of the Pharaoh during the 16th and 11th centuries BC, when the realm was at its height. Luxor Temple and Karnak Temple are two massive, well-known landmarks that are part of the city of Luxor today. The regal tombs known as the Valley of the Kings and the Valley of the Queens are located on the west bank of the River Nile. As there are so many attractions and landmarks, it is difficult to see them all in a short trip. In essence, the city is an outdoor exhibition hall and the ideal place in Egypt to showcase its ancient heritage.

Luxor is a remarkable location with a wide variety of sanctuaries and tombs, each with a unique history. The ancient city of Thebes is cited as the ideal location under the reign of the Middle Kingdom and New Kingdom pharaohs who created massive plans for burial grounds, secluded in the middle of the gritty backstreet of the Nile's West Bank. The magnificent panorama is only partially illustrated by the brilliant designs of the Karnak Temple complex. The sheer quantity of attractions where tourists can really take in the elegance and loftiness can take up a significant portion of the week-long excursion.

At Luxor, the Karnak sanctuary complex is regarded as an exceptionally noteworthy example of ancient Egyptian human advancement. Together with numerous other unique designs, the complex includes the Great Temple of Amun, the Temple of Khons, and the Festival Temple of Tuthmosis III. The complete complex focuses on the engineering advancements achieved by the forward-thinking Egyptian rulers, who enhanced this fantastic, verified structure with customary designs that consolidated the social advancements established during the New Kingdom era.

Gezira Island and Zamalek

Zamalek is the name of a district located in the northern part of Cairo. Located between Giza and Heliopolis, Zamalek is also home to Gezira Island.

The district today is still a very diverse place with peoples from all over the world coming to it for various reasons.

Founded in the early 19th century, the island was originally named for its location in the Nile River (ancient Egyptian for gift of the river), which forms a "gift" (in Arabic) shape. Gezira was used as a cotton plantation and later a club for elite residents of Cairo. It was also home to Gezira Sporting Club, which was founded in 1907 by British citizens and is one of the oldest sporting clubs in Egypt.

Gezira Island is the only island in Cairo. The ancient city of Beni Hasan was founded around the island, but the former island's mud walls were removed and became a neighborhood in Zamalek. The Giza lighthouse was built on Gezira in 1891 and served as a landmark on the way to Giza from any point within Cairo.

Islamic Cairo North

Islamic Cairo north is a small town north of Cairo, Egypt. It's extremely safe and it's also a great place to visit as well.

The people that live in Islamic Cairo north are friendly and welcoming. You will get the chance to see many different activities while visiting this small town. One thing that you might experience while visiting the Islamic Cairo north is how clean everything is. You will also see how people take care of the city as well.

By visiting this small town, you will be able to see how the Egyptian people take great pride on their city. Islamic Cairo north is one of the most important places in its area as it holds many tourist attractions and a museum as well. It's very easy to get to this small town from different parts of Cairo and it's just about a two-hour drive from the center of Cairo.

Food here is pretty cheap compared to other areas in Egypt.

Islamic Cairo South

The Islamic Cairo South has been developed over time to give visitors a sense of what life was like before modern times. Walking through the streets on this tour takes one back to the 19th century before solid structures covered with marble were erected on top of ancient buildings.

Today's Islamic Cairo South is an area where the ancient and modern cultures of Egypt mix. For example, these landmarks are still a vital part of local life, but they also make for very interesting photo opportunities for visitors. The Islamic Cairo South offers a wide variety of things to see and do, all of which can be found right in this section. Visitors to this area can also shop in the many markets, which are must-see. These markets sell everything from hand-made goods to fresh fruits and vegetables.

The Islamic Cairo South is the home of Egypt's largest mosque and it is located at the heart of the city. In November 624 A.D., Fustat was founded here, and since then it has been home to millions of people throughout history.

Alexandria

Semirames Hotel, El-Gaish Rd, Al Mesallah Sharq, Al Attarin (Tel: 20-3-48468370) $20.

Green Plaza Inn (5 stars), Alexandria Governorate, (Tel: 20-3-3830284) $35-40.

Alexander the Great Hotel, 5 Oskofia St, besides the Greek Church, $30.

Royal Crown Hotel, 159 Cornish Road, Cleopatra, Alexandria, $25.

Kaoud Sporting Hotel (Families Only), Geish Road 133, Alexandria, $10.

Chapter 5: - Luxor And The Nile Valley

Esna

Most visitors don't travel independently to see the temple at Esna, mostly because of its location. It lies 34 miles south of Luxor, 30 miles north west of Edfu and 86 miles north of Aswan so it isn't really convenient for a 'drop in'.

Esna tends to be a brief stop-over on a Nile cruise, normally *en route* from Aswan back to Luxor. The cruiseboat moors up at the edge of town and depending on the exact location, a short walk or a brief taxi ride will take visitors to the Temple of Khnum.

The original temple dates from the 18th dynasty and the reign of the Pharaoh Tuthmosis II but most of the present structure dates from the Greco-Roman period.

The first thing that strikes visitors is that the temple is about thirty feet below the present ground level. This is because once the temple was abandoned, it gradually filled with sand and debris and eventually it was almost entirely covered. The area was built over and the temple was buried.

Eventually the temple was partially uncovered again – it was used as a cotton warehouse in the mid-19th century AD – by which time the town had grown up around it.

Access to the temple is down a flight of modern metal steps into an open courtyard area and the temple is at the opposite end. The façade of the temple is 121 feet long and 49 feet high, the vestibule is 108 feet long and 54 feet wide and the 24 columns holding up the roof stand 37 feet high. Each design on the tops (capitols) of the columns is slightly different and some still show signs of the original paint. The ornate design of the capitols is common to the Greek and Roman period and not found in Ancient Egyptian temples.

Dendera

Dendera is a town in Egypt with ancient remains, including temples and pyramids. It is 48 kilometers south of the modern city of Luxor, just east of the Nile Valley. The site was one of the most prestigious in all Egypt.

Dendera is an ancillary temple for Hathor, Goddess of Beauty, Music and Dance at Denderah near Ancient Oasis Dendara. This priestess of Hathor was mistress of the Sycamore tree who nursed the infant Horus, and later became his first wife.

It is one of Egypt's largest temples and is comparable in size to Luxor Temple. The name Dendera may come from "Mutnedjmet", a reference to a goddess worshipped in the area later known as Dendera at Philae, where she was called "Mutnedjmet" ("she loved justice").

The Greek name "Nēdérá", means "City of columns." , which was Latinized as "Dendera" when the city became a Roman colony, is derived from the Egyptian phrase Djn-Tr ("holy dwelling"), which refers to a temple to Hathor at Philae.

Abydos

Abydos is a Paleolithic site in Upper Egypt. It's one of the most important archaeological sites in Egypt, because it provided direct evidence of early human activity.

Abydos was discovered in 1898 by François Auguste Ferdinand Mariette and later excavated by his assistant Émile Amélineau.

In the 1920s Ludwig Borchardt began to excavate Khentkaus I's tomb complex at Abydos, which included about fifty other tombs.

Abydos contains many archaeological finds; the best known is the tomb of Senebkay, a ruler predating king Scorpion.

El- kab

El-Kab is an archeological site in Egypt.

El-Kab is a town and commune of Al Qalyūbiya Governorate, the seat of one of several former kingdoms in Lower Egypt, located on the west bank Nile 60 km (37 miles) from Cairo. It is also known as El-kab or El-Keb.

The town was called "Sethroides" during ancient times.

The town is the location of a temple of Heryshef (Horus), the god of Lower Egypt, built during the Ptolemaic Period.

The town is first mentioned as "Sethroides" by Greek geographer Strabo in his book "Geographica", in which he mentions "Sethroides, a village at the Mount Hebo, on the road from Alexandria to Elephantine.

Luxor:

Cleopatra Hotel, $15-20 (3 star), Gezirat West Bank, Al Bairat (tel: 20-100-386 8345) http://www.cleopatrahotelluxor.com

Grand Hotel, $10-15, 11 minutes from Luxor Temple. (tel: 20-100-496-1848).

Ibrotel Luxor, $40 (4 stars), Khaled Ibn El Waleed Street.

Gaddis Hotel, $25, (2 stars), Khaled Ibn El Walid St.

Mercure Luxor Karnak, $38 to 45 depending upon rooms, with breakfast, (4 stars), 3 km from the open-air museum.

New Memnon Hotel, $35-40, www.newmemnonhotel.com

Gold Ibis Hotel, $20 (3 stars), Colossi of Memnon, Luxor West (tel: 20-95-2060984)

Rezeiky Hotel & Camp, $20 (3 stars), between Luxor Temple and Karnak Temple.

Pyramids of Luxor, $15-20 (3 stars) West Bank, Gezira Ramla Nile St.

Chapter 6: - Aswan And Lake Nasser

Aswan is the second largest city in Egypt, situated on the shore of this country's southernmost point, the Aswan High Dam on the Nile River. It was once home to an ancient Egyptian city of Upper and Lower Egypt, known today as Old Aswan. Situated across from a deep gorge that stretches several miles to the Red Sea coast, just north of Luxor; it also served as a trade route across Africa by camel.

The ancient city of Aswan is known today as Old Aswan. It was one of Egypt most important trading center situated on the Nile River and the Egypt. Old Aswan dates to around 3100 B.C in Egypt's Early Dynastic Period, when its first king named Scorpion ruled over Upper and Lower Egypt from his capital at the Unas-necropolis near the modern city of Edfu.

Aswan also played an important role in the early trade routes for gold and incense along the Nile River during pre-dynastic and dynastic times and continued to be a major center of trade in later times. It is also believed that the area of Aswan was home to ancient settlements during prehistoric times, although very few of them survived past the pre-dynastic era. The activities of a prehistoric community that existed at the time of the Giza pyramid builders at the beginning of Egypt's Old Kingdom is evidenced by large numbers of debris found in and around the city, including hundreds of pottery fragments from workshops. It is the earliest known archaeological evidence in Egypt. These settlements may have been inundated during later periods of lower water levels, but when digging at Aswan there has never been any indication to this effect.

There is also evidence of even earlier settlement at Aswan, dating back to around 5000 B.C. An ancient Egyptian town was located at Aswan in the Late Predynastic Period, but this site has not been located. However, it seems that the original town must have been founded before 5500 BC because some objects found there are older than this period's pottery, which usually only appears during the Protodynastic Period.

Lake Nasser

Lake Nasser, also known as Lake Nubia, is an artificial lake created by the building of the Aswan High Dam across the waters of the Nile at Aswan. The dam was constructed between 1960 and 1970 for a number of reasons:

It provides water for irrigation in Egypt's Nile valley and its evaporated output sustains a portion of Egyptian agriculture near Cairo; it generates electricity; and regulates river levels downstream. It regulates floods.

The lake is named after the Nubian king of Egypt, Nasser. The Egyptian actress Faten Hamama is often credited with suggesting the name to Nasser in 1955.

With a surface area of , Lake Nasser covers an area of . It lies in the Aswan Lowlands and has a depth. The dam's purpose is to provide for irrigation, electric power generation and flood control on the Nile River and its tributaries. It supplies water for 74 towns, villages and farms along the Nile's banks. The lake supplies drinking water to one million people and is the main source of irrigation for Egyptian agriculture. The lake also provides an important environmental habitat for a great diversity of fish and bird life.

The lake was created by building the Aswan High Dam across the waters of the Nile at Aswan, which is in southern Egypt about 200 km north of Cairo. The dam's purpose is to provide for irrigation, electric power generation and flood control on the Nile River and its tributaries.

Philae and the Temple of Isis

Everything about Philae is special and beautiful and much of it is unique.

Located about four miles south of Aswan, this beautiful temple stands on the former granite island of Agilkia surrounded by the Nile. It is one of the real success stories of the rescue operation to save as many temples as possible from the rising waters of Lake Nasser, following the construction of the Aswan High Dam in the 1960's.

Much of the temple had been submerged when the first Aswan Dam was built and sadly, the water washed away the glorious colours from the roof and columns. The colours of the temple can be seen in the paintings of British artist David Roberts, who travelled throughout Egypt in the 1800's and sketched most of the major sites.

There is a film called 'Valley of the Kings' which was made in 1954 and stars Robert Taylor and Eleanor Parker. It is interesting because it shows many of the important sites in Egypt - from the Pyramids of Giza to St Catherine's Monastery at Sinai, from the Valley of the Kings to Abu Simbel - as they were in the 1950's. At the end of the film one scene shows the couple in a felucca with the Temple of Isis at Philae in the background; the temple almost entirely submerged.

The name 'Philae' is Greek (a Greek corruption of the Egyptian word 'Pi-Lak') and it means 'pearl' and certainly, this is one of the jewels of Egypt. The temple is dedicated to the goddess Isis but her husband Osiris, their son Horus and the goddess Nephthys (the sister of Isis) were all worshipped here, too.

Tourists arrive at the jetty by coach, taxi or mini bus from Aswan and transfer to a motor boat for the few minutes it takes to reach the island. It is normal practice now that once on the boats, everyone has to wear lifejackets. It's probably a sensible safety precaution to wear bright orange, high visibility life jackets but they're a nightmare to accessorise!

As the southernmost temple of its kind in Ancient Egypt, the annual Nile flood would be detected here earlier than at the temples further north. The ancient Nilometer can still be seen at the site. A Nilometer consists of a series of stone steps leading down from the temple to the river and there were markings cut into the walls. As the water level rose and came up the steps, it could be measured by the marks.

Taxes were levied on crops so it was essential to know whether there was likely to be a flood (which could wash away the crops) or a drought (which would mean the crops could not be watered and would die) or whether there would be a normal harvest. Due to the importance of the temple in measuring the Nile's flood, the Nile gods Satet and Khnum were also worshipped here in ancient times.

I think Philae is one of the most beautiful temples in Egypt and it is also one of the most complete. In fact, it is more complete than it had been for decades because of the restoration carried out during the rescue operation.

Between 1972 and 1980, an Italian company – supported by Egyptian labourers – set about trying to save this unique temple and the way they did it was nothing short of amazing. The company – Condotti-Mazzi Estero – was contracted to carry out the work under the auspices of UNESCO and English and Egyptian consulting engineers.

This massive undertaking involved building a steel coffer dam around the site into which was pumped a million cubic meters of sand and water infill. The water drained out leaving the sand behind and the area just about high and dry. Pumps took care of the small quantities of water which leaked in.

Kom Ombo

Kom Ombo is an ancient temple which stands on the north western edge of El-Kom Ombo. The name means "placing oneself in the sand," and it is believed that those who came here to pray and pass their time would place themselves in the sand while they prayed. The name was given to the temple when it was discovered by archeologists during the first half of the 20th Century.

The temple is revered by Egyptians and foreigners alike. It is situated at the edge of a great lake, now known as Kom Ombo Lake. The lake has recently been drained as part of an effort to rebuild the city's infrastructure; however, Kom Ombo (meaning "Placing Oneself in Sand") still remains a place of worship for Egyptians, especially Coptic Christians.

In ancient times, the city of Kom Ombo was a place for worshiping two gods. They were Sobek, the crocodile god, and Haroeris, a falcon/sun god. It is said that a statue of Haroeris stood on the left side of the temple while Sobek's statue was on the right. To show respect to both gods, their statues faced each other with the Nile River running in between them.

Abydos Temple

The sanctuary of Osiris in the dusty town of Abydos is considered among the most entrancing imaginative old fortunes of antiquated Egypt. With lofty tall sections and dividers, the guests are hypnotized by the delightful hieroglyphics and multifaceted works of art. The sanctuary of Seti I at Abydos, additionally called the Great Temple of Abydos, is a fabulous legacy of antiquated Egypt, however he personally is viewed as one of the less popular New Kingdom pharaohs.

Because of the rule of Ramesses II, seemingly perhaps the best pharaoh, Seti I is a less popular pharaoh, yet his standard was an achievement in Egypt's set of experiences as he brought delay purchase to Egypt and laid out Egypt's sway over its eastern neighbors (present-day Syria and Levant district) again.

Al Anfushi

The opening of a new archaeological site at Al-Gouna, the first stage of a modern tourism project, has been held in this ancient city. All the findings have been assigned to their rightful places according to their original context and dating. In addition to that, the new site gives visitors an opportunity to explore and take part in archaeology with scientific accuracy as well as cultural understanding. Al-Gouna is located between Abu Simbel and Aswan on Egypt's western edge near the border with Sudan.

The new archaeological site includes the temple, an arch and a megalith. Beginning at the entrance, one can see a huge basalt rock which was previously ascribed to the Roman period, but according to investigations carried out by Prof. Dr Abd El-Latif El- Megloul from Aswan University, it dates to BCE.

The center of the complex has a huge limestone table which is decorated with multiple carved stones representing animals and humans.

Sharm el-Sheikh is a resort town between the desert of the Sinai Peninsula and the Red Sea. It is known for its sheltered sandy beaches, clear waters, and coral reefs. Diverse marine life and hundreds of Red Sea coral reef sites make Sharm El Sheikh a magnet for divers and eco-tourists.

The coastal line is fringed by white-sand beaches and swaying palm trees. Amongst the top beaches are Naama Bay, Jolanda Reef (divers flock here to explore the remains of the Jolanda, an old Cypriot freighter ship that ran aground in 1980), Ras Um Sid Beach and Reef, Jackson Reef. The fish life and enchanting coral gardens are the main attraction. Sharm el-Sheikh has many five-star hotels offering luxury lodging; prominent of them are Steignberger, Rixos Prium Seagate, Rixos Shar el-Sheikh, Sunrise Montemare Resort, Sunrise Arabian Beach, Le Royal Holiday, Four Seasons, Royal Savoy, La Branda Tower. The rates are flexible and vary according to the season and the size of the group.

Located 90 kilometers north of Sharm el-Sheikh, Dohab is regarded as the backpacker resort of Sinai and a good alternative to the usual travel package of Sharm el-Sheikh. The vast number of shoreline cafés and casual restaurants are lively places, while the shopping district near the highway has clusters of souvenir shops.

Between Egypt's mainland and the Sinai Peninsula lies the straits of Gubal. One of the ends of the Red Sea splits into two gulfs - Suez to the west and Aqaba to the east. The water here is shallower that has plenty of nutrient-rich currents flow that attracts a variety of marine life in all sizes and shapes. With shallow reefs and a large volume of shipping traffic passing through this area, the 19th and 20th centuries saw many accidents. Thus, the Gulf of Gubal is the best place for diving to explore the shipwrecks. Also, best for scuba diving, this place attracts adventure tourists. The guides on boats of diving safari can offer the best site for diving, including discovering old shipwrecks and the WW II memorabilia. The most famous shipwreck in the Red Sea area is that of SS Thilstlegorm. The other famous wrecks in the same direction are SS Dunraven, SS Ulysses, and SS Rosalie Moller, within just three kilometers of each other.

New Cairo

Welcome to Cairo! The largest city in the Middle East and Africa, this cosmopolitan capital is home to over 18 million people. With so much going on, it might be difficult to know where to start. To help you out, we've got your 5-day Cairo guide right here!

Day One: Visit the iconic Giza Plateau and take in the glory of built wonders such as the Sphinx and Great Pyramids. If you haven't had your fill of the pyramids, then make sure to visit the Cairo Museum. The Egyptian Museum has some incredible collections like Tutankhamun's tomb and Egyptian jewelry. It's one of the best museums in Cairo with a lot of unique artifacts. Other great sites to see in the city include the Hanging Church, Virgin Mary's Tree, Mohamed Ali Mosque and the Citadel.

Day Two: Peruse local artisan goods, handmade crafts at Khan ElKhalili Bazaar which is one of the most popular marketplaces in Old Cairo. Shop around and then take a break from all the shopping with a delicious meal at one of the many restaurants within this area. If you're interested in the performing arts, then head to the Cairo Opera House. Here, you can see a varied program of plays and performances. For those who are into shopping, Khan El Khalili is a great place to shop locally. The famous Khan El-Khalili Bazaar is one of the most popular markets in Old Cairo and is where many locals shop for all types of goods such as clothing, handicrafts, summer clothes and souvenirs.

Downtown Cairo

Opinions are mixed on Downtown Cairo because it is the capital of Arab art and culture. More than 850 galleries make this a hot destination for art lovers. There is also a lot of material here about Egyptian history, from pyramids to tombs to Islamic monuments. It's not all about workshopping though; there are plenty of opportunities for recreation in this bustling hub as well.

It is in the Downtown area, east of Tahrir Square, north and south of the Nile River.

Downtown Cairo is now an area which consists of a large retail center, government buildings and the palace of Muhammad Ali Pasha. There are many shopping malls, several large hotels and modern office buildings. The downtown has many restaurants, bars and nightclubs and a growing nightlife scene. It is considered to be the financial quarter of Cairo.

The historic city center is located on Tahrir Square. The famous Mausoleum of Egypt's first king, King Tutankhamun, is one of the most visited tourist destinations in Cairo. Nearby is the Giza Pyramids and Khan El Khalili bazaar. There are stores that sell artifacts from Old Egypt such as mummies and sphinxes, or modern Egyptian items like carpets and souvenirs.

Karnak temple

The Karnak temple is the most important, and some say the largest, of all Egyptian temples. The site's structure has been a keystone in building technology for about 1000 years.

After the conquest of Egypt by Alexander the Great, this temple became an important cult center for Ptolemaic kings until its invasion by Roman Emperor Augustus. It was one of six ancient world wonders, either built or confirmed as one by Antipater of Sidon in around 140 BC. The temple remained a center of worship for the Roman Empire. In the 19th century, the temple was used as a quarry for building work and fell into disrepair. Later, in 1831, it became an

Ottoman firing range and prison until 1983, when it was opened to tourists again.

A large rectangular sanctuary is surrounded by a wall with twelve gates on each side. The massive building structure is divided into three naves by two rows of pylons that stand on either side of an open court in front of them.

The citadel

The Citadel in Egypt, also known as the Egyptian Citadel or the Gayer-Anderson Castle, is a vast construction built by the Mamluk Sultanate at the beginning of their rule over Egypt. The Citadel became famous for its vast size and unique design with no parallel anywhere in Egypt.

It was built on a high natural point in Cairo overlooking both north and west of Cairo which suggests that it was intended as an answer to a defense need with respect to Cairo's strategic position. After the completion of the Citadel, it became the seat of government and residence for the sultans.

The Citadel was built on a site where a citadel had already existed during the Fatimid era, known as "Futuh" or "Kal'a al-Futuh " (Fortress), and later rebuilt by Salah al-Din Ayyubi in 1176.

Final Words

On final thought it is definitely worth it to visit Egypt and learn about the Egyptian culture and how the ancient Egyptians have developed over time. The magnificent structures may be the highlight of the trip but the diverse cultures is just as important. In the modern-day Egypt has become a Muslim country and the country is still doing its part in preserving the Christian heritage, the country has become a tourist Mecca for people from all over the world to visit and every person is trying to learn more and more about Egypt.

Made in the USA
Columbia, SC
25 June 2023

19241426R00028